Ward Lock's

Children's Encyclopedia

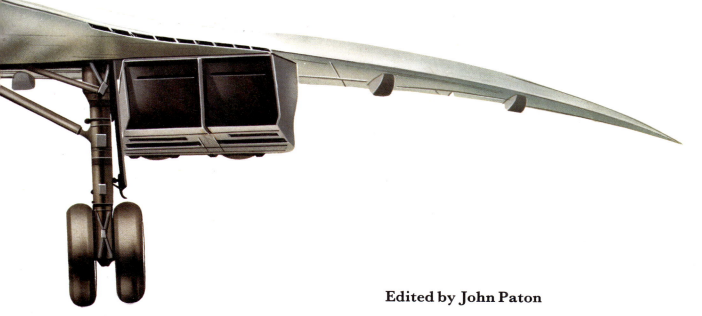

Edited by John Paton

Ward Lock Limited · London

Contents

MARE
IMBRIUM

OCEANUS
PROCELLARUM

Copernicus

MARE
NUBIUM

MARE
HUMORUM

First published in Great Britain 1976 by Ward Lock Limited,
116 Baker Street, London, W1M, 2BB.
Reprinted 1977
© Grisewood & Dempsey Limited 1976.

Designed and produced by Grisewood & Dempsey Limited, Elsley
House, 24-30 Great Titchfield Street, London, W.1.

Printed in Italy by Vallardi Industrie Grafiche, Milan.

ISBN 0 7063 5284 x

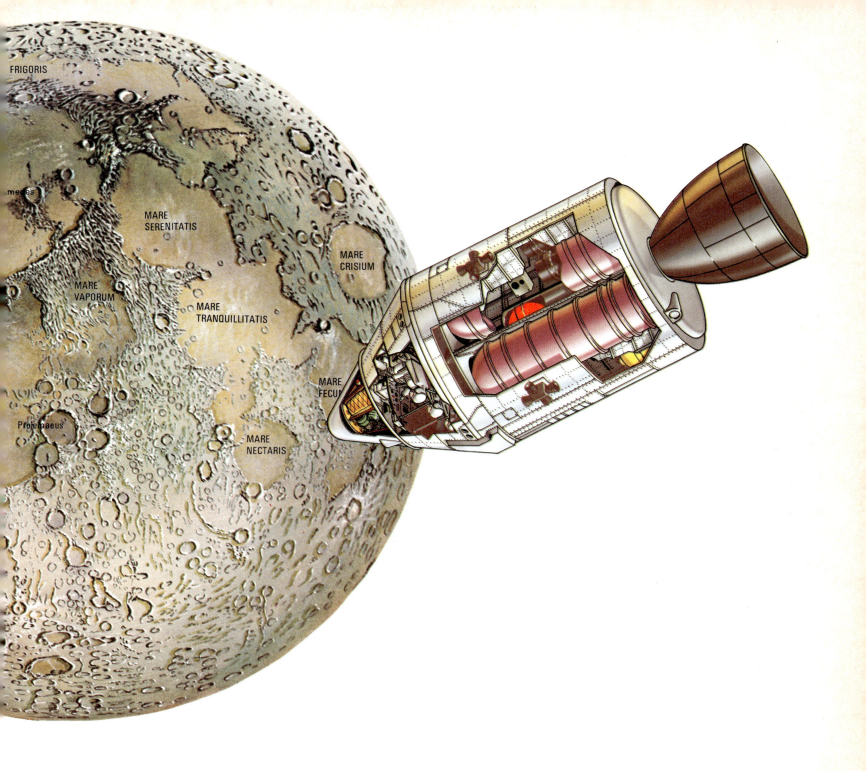

FRIGORIS

meres

MARE
SERENITATIS

MARE
VAPORUM

MARE
TRANQUILLITATIS

MARE
CRISIUM

MARE
FECU...

Ptolemaeus

MARE
NECTARIS

About this Book

Ward Lock's Children's Encyclopedia gathers together a mass of information in a new way. The book is divided into five main subjects: 'Our Wonderful World', 'Wonders of Life', 'Around the World', 'The Story of Man', and 'Here, There and Everywhere'. Open it at any page and you will find out new and fascinating facts about our world and its wonders.

Within the large subjects there are separate two-page sections —'Power from the Sun', 'Cold Lands', 'The Undersea World', etc. And within each two-page section there lie a host of related subjects.

Because the book has been arranged in this way, the index on page 61 is very important. If you want to find out where anything is, go to the index first. It will help you to get the most out of your encyclopedia.

Our Earth in Space

The earth is only a tiny speck among all the stars and planets. But it is our home and just right for us to live on.

Our earth seems very big to us, but it is just one of nine planets that move around the sun. The sun and everything that spins around it make up the 'Solar System'.

This is the earth as a spaceman sees it.

A Lot of Suns

A famous astronomer once said that there are more stars like our sun in the universe than there are grains of sand on all the beaches in the world. Yet all these stars are very far apart. Our own sun has lots of room to move about in. Its nearest star neighbour is 40,000 million kilometres away. It has been said that if there were only three kangaroos in Australia the country would be more crowded with kangaroos than space is with stars.

Here is the earth moving round and round the sun with eight other planets.

Our sun is much bigger than all its planets put together. It is also very, very hot. But our sun is just a star – a very ordinary star. It is two-thirds of the way from the centre of a whole cluster of stars called a 'galaxy'. At night we can see it as the Milky Way.

On the right is our vast galaxy of stars. The sun and its planets are the speck of light at the point of the arrow. But there are millions of galaxies. Our whole huge galaxy is only a speck among them (below).

But this galaxy of stars – our galaxy – is only one of millions of galaxies. Some of these galaxies are so far away the light from them has taken over 5,000 million years to reach us.

All this shows how small our earth is in the vast universe. But to man it is a perfect home. It is the only planet in the Solar System with the right temperature and atmosphere to allow men to live.

Among the millions of unseen planets out in space there must be others with conditions like the earth's. On these planets there must be beings who may, one day, get a message through to us.

The picture above is a small part of the Bayeux Tapestry. The tapestry was embroidered on a strip of linen 70 metres long and shows the conquest of England by the Normans in 1066. This piece shows people pointing in astonishment at Halley's Comet. The picture on the right shows what the comet looked like when it last appeared in 1910.

What are Stars?

The stars we see in the night sky are like our sun. But they look small because they are very far away. Some are smaller than our sun. Others are hundreds of times bigger.

The stars seem to move across the sky. But it is the earth that is moving. The earth spins like a top. It also travels around the sun.

Scientists think that stars are made from clouds of gas and dust. A star begins to shine when atomic explosions start inside it, making it very hot. Our sun shines because there are always vast numbers of huge explosions, just like hydrogen bomb explosions, going on inside it.

Comets and Shooting Stars

Comets are big balls of dust and gas that travel through space. They travel round the sun, just like the planets. As you can see from the picture above, they have long glowing tails. This is Halley's Comet which can be seen from earth every 76 years. It was last seen in 1910 and will be seen again in 1986.

Meteors are pieces of rock that journey round the sun. We cannot see them until they enter the earth's blanket of air. Then they glow white hot as they streak through the night sky. They are also called 'shooting stars'.

Meteors usually burn up before they reach the ground. But sometimes big ones do hit the earth.

Huge radio telescopes like the ones on the right receive signals sent out by stars too far away to be seen by ordinary telescopes. They are also used to track spacecraft.

The Air Around Us

The earth is covered by a blanket of air which stretches upwards for a few hundred kilometres. Without this 'blanket' there would be no living creatures on earth. Our planet would be a barren world like the moon, boiling hot all day and freezing cold each night.

The Air is Vital

Without air we could not breathe. But air is vital to us in other ways. It helps shield us from dangerous rays that come in from outer space. Like a blanket, it keeps the earth warm at night and shields us from the sun's fierce heat during the day.

The air also allows us to hear things. Sound waves travel in the air. Without air we would have to talk to each other by radio, as astronauts have to do on the moon.

Our blanket of air is also called the *atmosphere*.

Air and No Air

If you look at the pictures on these pages you will see how small a distance above and below the earth's surface we move in. Imagine that the top of this page is about 160 kilometres above sea level. There is hardly any air up there. The mountain below is Everest, the highest in the world. Birds cannot fly as high as Everest.

The big Jumbo jet plane is flying at 10,000 metres. The fast-flying Concorde is flying at 17,000 metres. There is not enough air for people to breathe at the height these planes fly at. So the planes have to take their own air supply with them.

The dark blue area below shows the deepest part of the sea – 11,000 metres below sea level.

Air Has Weight

Air can be weighed. If you weigh an 'empty' bottle, you are weighing both the bottle and the air inside it. Pump the air out of the bottle and weigh it again. It will be lighter. The difference between the first and second weight is the weight of the air that was in the bottle.

On the right you can see the earth, surrounded by its blanket of air. The air gets thinner and thinner the higher one goes. At a height of 500 kilometres there is hardly any air at all.

Air presses on everything. To show this, take a glass of water and place a card over the top (left). Turn the glass upside down (centre). When you take your hand away (right) the card stays in place. This shows that the air pressure beneath is greater than the weight of the water.

High on Mount Everest the air is so thin, men have to wear oxygen masks.

The Air Above Us

Our earth is unlike other planets in the sun's system in many ways. But perhaps the most important difference is that it is surrounded by air. Compared to the size of the earth, this layer of air is not very thick. It goes upwards from the earth's surface for only a few hundred kilometres. And about half of all the earth's air is pulled into the 7 kilometres closest to the surface. Above this the air is so thin, men cannot move about easily without wearing oxygen masks.

At a height of 500 kilometres there is hardly any air at all.

Why is the Sky Blue?

The sky is blue because the sun's light has to shine through our atmosphere. Sunlight is a mixture of light of all colours. Our atmosphere is made up of air, dust, and tiny particles of water. As sunlight passes through, its blue light is scattered more than its other colours. This scattered light we see as blue sky.

Floating on Air

The hovercraft above is floating on a cushion of air. In fact, hovercraft are often called air cushion vehicles. They are something between a ship and a plane. Powerful jet engines push air downwards through the bottom of the craft. This air lifts the craft off the water. It can then skim over the surface of the waves very quickly, pushed by propellers like a plane. It can also travel over land.

The hovercraft above is carrying cars and people at 100 kilometres per hour between England and France.

Rubbing Against Air

When anything rubs against anything else there is what we call *friction*. Friction makes things hot. Rub your hands together hard. They get hot. When you rub a match against a matchbox, so much heat is made the match bursts into flame.

When things go through air they get hot too. Fast planes have to be made of special metal that doesn't melt from the heat. When spacemen come back to earth in their space capsule (above) they whizz through our air at a terrific speed. The front of the space capsule has to be made of a very special material that burns away slowly in the great heat caused by the air.

The highest layer of the atmosphere is called the 'ionosphere'. Beyond it lies empty space. In the ionosphere the atoms in the air are electrified by streams of particles coming in from space. These electrified atoms are very useful to us. They reflect radio waves back to earth a long way away. So we can send radio waves round the earth by bouncing them off the ionosphere.

We think of clouds being very high in the sky. But very few of them are as high as Mount Everest. The highest clouds are the streaky cirrus, and these are not found very often above 15,000 metres.

The highest a man has flown is about 36 kilometres. Helicopters can fly as high as 10,000 metres (right).

Man first rose off the ground because hot air rises. In 1783 the Montgolfier brothers in France filled a cloth bag with hot air. It rose several thousand metres into the air with two men aboard (left).

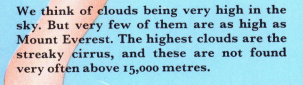

Our Neighbour, the Moon

The moon is our nearest neighbour in space. It is only 390,000 kilometres away, which is quite close when we think that the sun is nearly 400 times further away.

We Only See One Face

We can call the moon 'our moon' because it really does belong to us. It is a *satellite* of our earth and makes a complete circle round us in a month. The moon itself is also spinning. It takes it a month to make one spin. This means that we always see the same face of the moon from earth. It was only when we were able to send spacecraft round the moon that we found out what the back of our neighbour was like. And it was found that the back is very much like the face we see from earth.

Moonlight is Really Sunlight

When we look at the full moon on a clear night we are often surprised how brightly it shines. But the moon is not giving out any light at all. All it is doing is reflecting light from the sun.

The picture below shows what happens. Sunshine is coming in from the left. It hits one side of the earth and one side of the moon. Standing on the dark side of earth we can look up and see the sunlight shining on the moon.

How Big is the Moon?

Very few people can guess how big the moon is. Because we see it in the sky looking as big as the sun, we think it is bigger than it really is. The moon is not very big. In fact, it is almost exactly the same size as Australia, as you can see in the picture above.

The moon is so small it cannot hold an atmosphere around it as the earth does. There is no air to breathe on the moon, so spacemen have to take their own air with them.

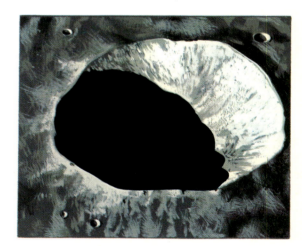

The Strange Craters

It has been known for hundreds of years that the moon's surface is covered with strange circles. These are called *craters*, and some of them are 300 kilometres across. The picture above shows one close up. It is thought that the craters have been caused by volcanoes.

The Moon's Eclipse

The earth travels round the sun and the moon travels round the earth. Sometimes the sun, the earth and the moon come in line with each other. Then the moon is eclipsed by the earth's shadow. You can see this in the picture below. The sun's light is coming in from the right. The light cannot reach the moon because the earth is in the way.

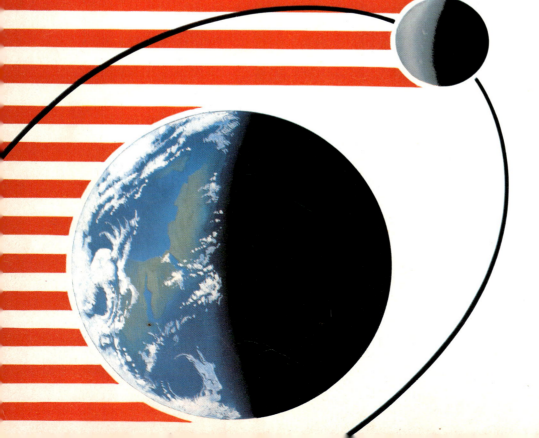

The picture on the left shows the moon as you would see it through a large telescope. You can see the craters. And there are also big dark areas. People used to think these dark areas were seas on the moon. They gave them names like 'Sea of Rains' and 'Ocean of Storms'. But now we know that there are no seas on the moon. The dark areas are just dry, flat plains. The moon has no water. It is a dry, lifeless place. There is no rain, no wind, no clouds, no weather.

Moon soil collected by the spacemen was made up of tiny pieces of rock and glass.

It is thought that many small craters on the moon have been made by meteors.

Men on the Moon

Men first stepped on to the moon in the year 1969. They were doing something very strange – something no man had ever done before.

Why was stepping on the moon so strange? First of all, there was no air there. The spacemen had to carry their own air in containers on their backs. And because there was no air, the spacemen couldn't speak to each other, no matter how loudly they shouted through their helmets. Sound needs air to travel through. They had to speak to each other by radio.

And the spacemen had to be very careful how they walked. Because the moon is so small, things on its surface weigh only a sixth of what they do on earth. And this includes spacemen.

A Very Hot World

The spacemen had also to wear specially cooled suits. Without them they would have burned up in the fierce heat on the moon's surface. Because there is no atmosphere on the moon, the sun's rays beat down with nothing to stop them. The temperature can rise to over 120°C.

The picture above shows the spacemen landing on the moon, with the earth shining down out of a black sky. On the left is the *Lunar Rover* which later spacemen used to drive about the moon.

The picture on the right shows the American spaceman Neil Armstrong. He was the first man to step on to the moon's dusty surface.

Power from the Sun

Nearly all the power we use comes from the sun. It may seem surprising that coal and oil are made by the sun. But indeed they are. Without the sun there would be no water power either. Even when you run you are using power from the sun.

Fuel from Plants

Coal is sometimes called a *fossil fuel*. This is because it was formed millions of years ago when the earth was covered with swamps. Huge fern-like plants grew then. When the plants died they fell into the swamps and decayed. Heat and pressure over many, many years changed the plants into coal. The mud of the swamps turned slowly into solid rock.

Coal is found in strips or *seams*. Miners dig it out as they are doing in the picture on the right. Men and machines rip out the coal. It is then taken in trucks to the main shaft. From there it is sent up to the surface.

Black Gold

Oil, like coal, was formed a long, long time ago from the remains of animals and plants. These animals and plants lived in the seas and were buried in layers of sand and mud. After millions of years heat and pressure turned them into oil that was trapped between layers of rock.

Now oilmen drill for oil by setting up tall derricks on land or at sea (picture right). They drill deep into the earth, sinking pipes in the hole. When the oilmen strike oil it usually flows to the surface by itself.

The crude oil is taken from the oil wells to *refineries*. It goes by pipeline or in big tanker ships. At the refinery it is turned into different kinds of oil – from thick, heavy oils to petrol for cars. Oil is sometimes called black gold.

Wind Power

No one knows who invented the windmill. As long ago as the 12th century people were using them to grind corn. The picture shows an old-fashioned Dutch windmill and a modern American windmill.

Muscle Power

When we run, our muscle power comes from the sun, too. Plants get their energy from the sun – they could not grow without the sun's light. Animals eat plants – the cow eats grass, for instance. We eat animals and plants, and from them we get energy to work our muscles. When we run we are using sun power.

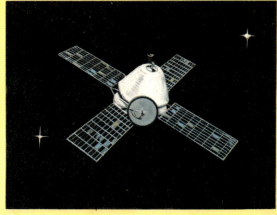

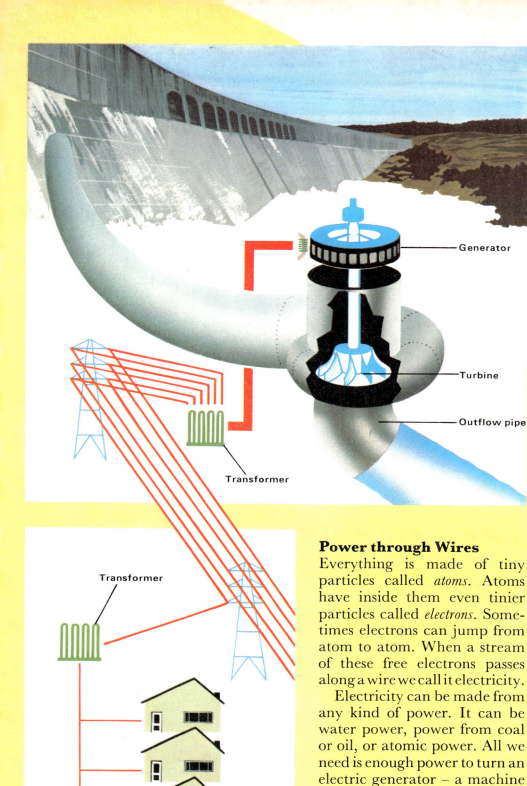

Generator

Turbine

Outflow pipe

Transformer

Transformer

Rain Power

Without the sun there would be no rain. It is rain that fills lakes and rivers with water. Without rain there would be no waterfalls. And the power of waterfalls can be used to make electricity.

More often, an artificial waterfall is made by damming a river or lake. Water builds up behind the dam. It can then be sent through big pipes and made to spin huge water *turbines* like the one in the picture. The turbines generate electricity. This electricity goes through a *transformer* which builds up the voltage of the electricity. This makes it easier to send the electricity through the grid wires all over the country. Before the electricity reaches our homes the voltage is brought down again.

Water power stations cost more to build than coal or oil power stations. But they are much cheaper to run. They do not need any fuel.

As coal and oil grow scarcer we will probably have to make more and more of our electricity from the power of falling water.

Power through Wires

Everything is made of tiny particles called *atoms*. Atoms have inside them even tinier particles called *electrons*. Sometimes electrons can jump from atom to atom. When a stream of these free electrons passes along a wire we call it electricity.

Electricity can be made from any kind of power. It can be water power, power from coal or oil, or atomic power. All we need is enough power to turn an electric generator – a machine that makes electricity. From the generator electricity is fed along wires to our homes and factories.

Power from the Atom

We all know that when an atom bomb explodes a huge amount of energy is let loose. There is an enormous amount of heat, light and noise. In atomic power stations we can now control atomic explosions. We can slow up the explosions and use the heat to make steam, just as we do in an oil power station. The steam drives big turbines which can be used to make electricity.

There is only so much coal and oil in the world. After a while these precious substances will be all used up. When they are, we will have to rely much more on atomic power.

Power in Space

When satellites are shot into space they have a job to do. They have to send back to earth information about the weather. Or they have to handle radio and television programmes and send them to the far corners of the world. The power for these jobs comes from the sun. The four wings of the spacecraft on the left hold hundreds of cells. These cells turn the sun's light into electricity. The electricity gives the satellite its power. This spacecraft was sent to Mars.

The Sun's Heat

A greenhouse is warm inside. Most people think that the glass has done something to the sun's rays to heat it up. This is not so. The rays pass right through the glass. They heat up everything in the greenhouse. The heat rays from things in the greenhouse are then trapped and cannot easily get out through the glass. So the greenhouse heats up.

Before and After the Dinosaurs

Before people lived on the earth, it was the home of many fantastic creatures. Dinosaurs ruled our planet for more than 100 million years – fifty times longer than we have been here.

Some of the creatures that lived in the sea before the first land animals appeared.

Labels on image: Water plants, Sponges, Trilobite, Jellyfish, Sea Scorpion, Nautiloid, Ammonite, Armoured fish, Fish with leglike fins, Early amphibian

Stone Bones
We know about the animals that lived before people were there to see them from fossils. Fossils are the remains of animals that have been preserved in the rocks. When they died, the soft parts of their bodies decayed but the bones sank into the mud and were buried. Lying hidden in the ground they slowly turned to stone. Millions of years later people found the stone bones, chipped them from the rocks, and put them all back together exactly as they would have been when the animal was alive. By looking at animals that are alive today, we can even tell what the outside of their bodies must have looked like.

Life in the Sea
About 600 million years ago the first living things appeared in the sea. Tiny plants and soft creatures, like little blobs of jelly, were wafted about by the waves. Soon the sea was full of animals. Trilobites crawled over the sea bed feeding on smaller creatures. Huge sea scorpions seized other animals in their long, sharp claws and giant octopus-like creatures strangled passing victims with tentacles that poked out from their hard shells. The first fishes had thick armour that protected them from the sea scorpions.

From Fins to Feet
The first living things on land were plants that grew along the water's edge. Fishes swam into the shallows to eat the insects that crawled over the plants. Some of the fishes could breathe out of water and they had strong fins which they could use as legs. On land there were no enemies to eat them, so they stayed there and slowly they changed into amphibians – the first land animals. But they could not go far from the water because they needed water to lay their eggs in.

Brontosaurus, a giant plant-eater.

Plesiosaur

Ichthyosaur

Pteranodon was a flying reptile that caught fish in its great beak.

Tyrannosaurus, the fiercest of all dinosaurs.

The Dreaded Dinosaurs

The first animals that could lay eggs on land were the reptiles. The greatest of all the reptiles were the dinosaurs. The name dinosaur means 'terrible lizard', but though many dinosaurs were enormous not many were terrible. Most of them were peaceful plant-eaters. Brontosaurus weighed 30 tonnes and was more than 20 metres long, but it could only plod slowly and had to spend nearly all its time eating to fill its huge stomach.

The fiercest of the dinosaurs was a meat-eater called Tyrannosaurus. It stood six metres high and ran on its huge back legs. It used the big claws on its small front legs for gripping its prey while it sank its dagger-like teeth into the flesh.

The Death of the Dinosaurs

Dinosaurs ruled the world for more than 100 million years. Then suddenly they died out. Nobody knows why, but many scientists think that the world became too cold for them. The animals that took their place were mammals. They had hair to keep them warm and were the most intelligent of all animals.

Two armoured plant-eating dinosaurs. Stegosaurus defended itself by swinging its spiked tail like a club. Triceratops charged its enemies with its horns.

Archaeopteryx was the first known bird. It evolved from the reptiles and was like a reptile in many ways. It had teeth in its beak, scales on its head and claws on its wings. And even though it had feathers, it could not fly very well.

The hairy mammoth was a mammal that lived during the Ice Age after the dinosaurs had died out.

The Undersea World

Men have explored nearly all the land surface of the earth. Only now are they beginning to find out about the vast world below the surface of the seas.

Men are going deeper and deeper into the strange, dark depths. Skin divers (1) can go down more than 60 metres. Divers wearing helmets and with air pipes to the surface (2) can reach below 150 metres. Ordinary submarines can cruise at 600 metres. A very special submarine called a bathyscaphe (3) has been down about 11,000 metres (11 kilometres). But going down very deep is not easy. Men have to be well protected against the enormous crushing pressure of the water. And, of course, they have to take their own air and light with them. It is completely black in the depths.

Deep Sea Fish

The fish of the deep ocean are very strange creatures. Most of them have huge mouths and sharp teeth with which they attack anything they meet. Fish like the deep-sea angler (4) lure other fish into their jaws with a small light on the end of a rod on top of their head. Others have patterns of lights along their sides (5 and 6). These lights help the fish to recognize each other in the dark. Some of the deep-sea fish are very long and thin. The snipe eel (7) is one of these. But none of the deep-sea creatures is very large. They are mostly small shrimp-like animals (8).

The Middle Waters

To find really big creatures we have to move up to the middle waters of the sea. There is the colourful roosterfish (9), which can be 5 metres long, and the fierce Moray eel (10). But the biggest by far are the whales. We know that sperm whales (11) battle in the deep waters with giant squids (12). These huge creatures can have tentacles over 7 metres long and as thick as a man's thigh.

The Top Level

In shallow waters we find the sharks (13), the sawfish (14), and the swordfish (15). The tuna (16) is caught and used as food. But the main food fish are those like the herring and the cod which are caught in large numbers by trawlers (17). Other fish in the picture are the huge, but harmless, manta ray (18), the fun-loving dolphin (19) and the curious sunfish (20). Leaping from the surface are the flying fish (21) found in tropical waters. They have been seen to stay in the air for as long as 40 seconds.

The World of Plants

Plants make up a very large and important part of nature. There are more than 360,000 kinds of plants. Some plants are so small that they can only be seen through a microscope. Others are over 100 metres tall and may live for thousands of years. Without plants there would be no life on Earth. They use sunlight to make food and energy from the soil. Animals can then get their food by eating plants. Some of these animals are, in turn, eaten by other animals.

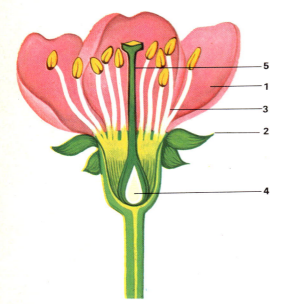

The Parts of a Flower

1. The *petals* are often brightly coloured to attract insects.

2. The *sepals* are like small leaves under the petals. When the flower was a bud, the sepals were on the outside to protect it.

3. The male parts (*stamens*) produce pollen in small containers (*anthers*) on the ends of long stalks.

4. The female part has a chamber (*ovary*) that contains the egg. The seed eventually grows here.

5. The stalk (*stigma*) on the top of the ovary receives pollen from the stamens of another flower.

Autumn berries are a useful supply of food for birds. But when the birds take the berries, they are also helping the plant. They help to spread the seeds by carrying them far away.

How Plants Produce Seeds

Flowers are needed so that plants can produce seeds. These eventually grow into new plants. In this way, plants make sure that their kind continues to exist.

The first stage in making a seed is called *pollination*. Pollen is taken from the anthers of one flower to the stigma of another. Some plants are pollinated by the wind. The wind blows pollen from one flower to another.

Most plants, however, are pollinated by insects. On a sunny day you can see many insects, especially bees and butterflies, flitting from one flower to the next. They are attracted by the bright colour of the petals and by the scent of nectar. When an insect enters the flower to drink the nectar, it brushes against the anthers and picks up pollen on its body. The insect then flies to another flower, where it leaves some of the pollen stuck to the top of the stigma.

One pollen grain on the stigma now produces a thin tube. This grows down through the stigma until it reaches the ovary. Here, the male cell of the pollen joins up with the female egg cell. This is called fertilization. The ovary, with the fertilized egg inside it, then grows into a seed.

All plants need water, but some plants actually grow in water. Water lilies, bulrushes and duckweed are all water plants that grow in ponds or slow-moving streams.

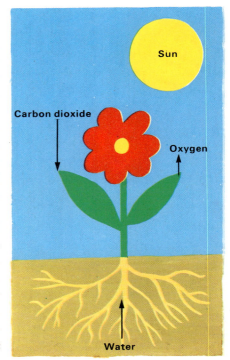

Food and Water

A plant makes its food using sunlight and carbon dioxide, which is one of the gases in the air. The leaves of a plant are green because they contain a material called chlorophyll. Carbon dioxide enters the leaves. The sunlight acts with the chlorophyll to turn carbon dioxide and water into plant food. At the same time oxygen comes out of the leaves. This is useful to animals because it is the gas they breathe.

A plant gets its water from the soil. It enters the roots and passes up the stem. Any water that the plant does not need passes out of the leaves.

Mushrooms and toadstools are unusual plants. They are not green because they do not contain any chlorophyll. Unlike green plants, therefore, they cannot make their own food. They have to get their food from rotted material in the ground.

Above: Giant redwood trees are conifers that grow in California in the United States. Some of the redwoods are several thousand years old and have grown more than 100 metres tall.

Left: Plants and their products have many uses. Paper is made from wood. Rubber is made from latex – the sap of the rubber tree. Some flowers are used in the making of perfumes. Plant fibres, such as cotton and flax, are used to make materials and string. Some plants contain substances that are used in medicines. Many plants are grown for their roots, stems, leaves or fruits, which are then eaten. The seeds of some grasses, such as wheat, are used to make bread.

Spreading the Seeds

Plants often make large numbers of seeds. When they are ready, they must be spread over as wide an area as possible. This is so that each seed will have the best possible chance of growing into a new plant.

Many plants have extremely clever ways of making sure that their seeds travel as far as possible. Poppy seeds are shaken, a few at a time, from a capsule that is rather like a pepper pot. The seeds are small and light and can be carried quite far by the wind. Dandelion seeds have tiny parachutes that allow the wind to carry them even

farther. Sycamore seeds have wings so that, instead of falling straight to the ground, they float away from the tree as they fall.

Many seeds are spread by animals. Burrs are fruits that have tiny hooks. When an animal brushes against the plant, the burrs, with the seeds inside them, catch onto the animal's fur. They may then be carried a long way before dropping off. Other fruits are attractive – to animals as well as humans. Many berries are picked from plants by birds. The seeds inside the berries may be carried for many miles before being dropped.

Animals and plants are useful to each other. Bees and butterflies find nectar in flowers. At the same time, they pollinate the flowers, which can then make seeds. Rabbits eat plants and are usually thought of as pests. But, by carrying seeds in their fur, they help to spread plants across the countryside.

Insects and Spiders

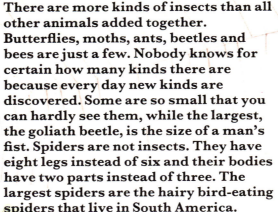

There are more kinds of insects than all other animals added together. Butterflies, moths, ants, beetles and bees are just a few. Nobody knows for certain how many kinds there are because every day new kinds are discovered. Some are so small that you can hardly see them, while the largest, the goliath beetle, is the size of a man's fist. Spiders are not insects. They have eight legs instead of six and their bodies have two parts instead of three. The largest spiders are the hairy bird-eating spiders that live in South America.

The scorpion is a relative of the spider. It runs very fast and catches its prey with its strong claws. Then it poisons the victim with the sting in the end of its tail.

A hoverfly trapped in the web of a garden spider.

If you go out into the countryside and look carefully, you will see many of the insects in this picture. If you see a bumblebee like this one carrying loads of red pollen on its legs, you will know that it has been feeding at its favourite flower, the red clover.

A damsel fly

A grasshopper

A plant-eating bug.

Two ants 'talking' to each other.

A Closer Look at Insects

Insects do not have skeletons inside their bodies like ours. They have a hard outer case to protect them. The three parts of their bodies are jointed so that they can move easily and their six legs also have joints. Most insects also have two pairs of wings. Some are big and beautiful like a butterfly's. Others are stiff and strong like a beetle's. Insects normally have two feelers on their heads. They use them mostly to smell and find their way about. Ants also use them to 'talk' to each other by rubbing them together.

If you look closely at an insect's eyes, you will see that they are very different from our own. Their eyes are made up of hundreds of tiny cone-shaped 'lenses'. Each one looks in a slightly different direction and works like a separate eye. The result is that objects look blurred to insects even though they can sense movement very well.

The crab spider has a cunning way of catching its food. It waits in a flower and seizes visiting insects. The insects have no chance of seeing it there because its body is exactly the same colour as the petals of the flower.

A monarch butterfly and its caterpillar.

The ladybirds' bright colour warns other animals that they are poisonous to eat.

Male stag beetles fight together for the females with their big antlers.

Animal Life Stories

Butterfly · Dragonfly · Bee · Salmon · Daddy longlegs · Frog

Different kinds of animals have very different life stories. The young of a mammal grows inside the mother's body until it reaches a certain size. When it is born, it looks like an adult, except that it is smaller and more helpless. But a caterpillar, which is the young of a butterfly, looks nothing like the adult. Like many insects it must go through a great change (called metamorphosis) before it becomes an adult butterfly. Not all insects, however, need to go through this great change during their life story. The young of the silverfish (shown above) looks like its parent when it emerges from the egg. It then just grows until it reaches the adult size.

The pictures above show the adults of six animals, and their young are below. Read the life stories on this page and try to guess which young belong to which adults. The young dragonfly is on the left.

Honey bees make a nest that consists of thousands of compartments (1). The queen bee lays eggs in empty compartments (2). An egg hatches out into a grub. This lives inside its compartment, where it is fed by adult bees (3). After a while, it changes into a pupa (4). Eventually, the insect emerges from the pupa as a fully grown adult (5).

A butterfly lays its eggs on the underneath of leaves (1). When the egg hatches, a caterpillar emerges. It feeds first on the leaf where the egg was laid, and then moves on to other leaves (2).

After a few weeks it finds a suitable place to rest, forms a hard case over itself (3), and becomes a chrysalis or pupa (4). Inside the chrysalis a great change takes place. Eventually the adult

butterfly breaks open the top of the case, and starts to emerge (5, 6). When it is completely out of the case it rests for a while until its wings unfold.

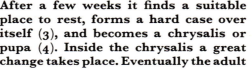

A salmon lays its eggs in the shallow water of streams far inland (1). Very young salmon are called fry (2), which live among the stones of the stream.

When they have grown larger, they are called parr (3). The parr swim downstream to the sea, where they become adult salmon (4). When it is

time for the breeding season to begin again, the adult salmon swim back up the rivers, sometimes leaping up waterfalls (5).

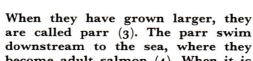

A frog lays its eggs on weed in ponds and streams (1). After a while a tadpole hatches out of the egg (2). For a few weeks the tadpole has fringe-like organs (called gills) on the outside of

its body. These are used for taking in oxygen from the water (3). As the tadpole grows, it loses its outside gills (4). After about three months, the tadpole goes through a series of

remarkable changes. The most obvious change is that legs develop (5, 6). Gradually the tail disappears. The adult frog is now able to leave the water and climb on to the land (7).

Reptiles

Most reptiles lay eggs with hard shells. They do not look after their young. In fact the parents of most reptiles are not usually around when the eggs hatch. Turtles lay their eggs on sandy beaches. They bury them under the sand and then leave them. Alligators, on the other hand, make a rough kind of nest. The mother lays her eggs and then waits until the young are ready to hatch. She then helps them to emerge by breaking the shells.

Birds

Like the reptiles, birds also lay eggs. Many birds build nests in which to lay their eggs. But the great difference between birds and reptiles is that birds look after both the eggs and the young.

An egg is laid while the young bird is growing inside. It gets its food from the yolk of the egg. The shell of the egg allows air to pass through into a space at one end. Blood vessels carry oxygen from this space to the growing bird.

Eggs are kept warm by the female bird, who sits on them until they hatch. Sometimes the male bird also takes a turn at sitting on the nest. When the eggs hatch, the young birds are completely helpless. The parents spend most of their time searching for food, to feed their young. When the young birds are old enough, they leave the nest and fly away.

Mammals

All mammals take great care of their young. The mother feeds the young with her milk and continues to look after them until they are able to fend for themselves.

The most primitive mammals are called *Monotremes*. There are only two kinds – the duck-billed platypus and the spiny anteater. They are the only mammals that lay eggs.

Marsupials are more advanced mammals. They include kangaroos, koala bears, and possums. The young grow inside the mother's body. But they are born in a very weak state. After birth, they crawl through the mother's fur until they reach the pouch, where they remain for some time.

The true mammals vary a great deal in shape, size, and way of life. They include humans, cats, dogs, rabbits, mice and whales. But they all have one main thing in common. The young are kept inside the mother's body until they they have grown to a considerable size.

Animal Friends and Enemies

In the savage world of nature, where the hunter often becomes the hunted, animals wage a constant battle to eat but not be eaten themselves.

For plant-eaters, finding food is not normally difficult. But not becoming food themselves often is. Most animals flee from their enemies. Only a few stand their ground and fight, and they normally have protective horns or armour.

For meat-eaters, finding food is more difficult simply because their victims always do their best to escape. To catch food they need speed and skill. A lion must quietly stalk its victim without letting the hunted animal catch its scent. And it must close in swiftly for the kill.

Everyone knows how difficult it is to catch a fly. Imagine how much more difficult it must be for a fish. Yet the archer fish has no trouble. It brings down flies by shooting a jet of water droplets at them as they fly over the surface or crawl on the waterweeds.

Low Cunning

For both hunter and hunted, cunning is often of more use than speed. The garden spider makes a web of sticky silk and sits in a nearby hideaway to wait for its victims to walk or fly into the trap. The praying mantis keeps per-fectly still as it waits in leaves as green as its body. Neither its victims nor its enemies know that it is there.

Many insects are protected by their colour or by their shape. There are moths that look like bark or dead leaves, caterpillars like pine needles, mantises like flowers, leaf insects like leaves, tree hoppers like thorns and stick insects like thin twigs. They look so like the plants they live on that their enemies pass them by without a second glance.

Safety in Numbers

Often living and feeding together is the safest way for animals to live. A meat-eater would rather attack an animal on its own than take on a whole herd. And in a herd, too, there are more animals to watch and warn the others when danger threatens. Some animals hunt together. In the Arctic, packs of wolves search for weak or wounded musk oxen to attack. But the musk oxen have a good defence. They herd the young ones together and form a tight circle around them. With their horns lowered they face the howling wolves who soon give up and go away.

As soon as it feels its prey touch the web, the garden spider rushes out of hiding, wraps the victim in silk and digs its poisonous fangs into the animal's helpless body.

The archer fish stuns its prey with a jet of water, shot with an aim as swift and sure as an archer's.

A herd of zebra gallop away from a hunting lioness. Without a good start, they could not possibly outrun her powerful strides. Their safety hangs only on the chance that she will tire first.

Protecting their young, a herd of musk oxen stand their ground against a pack of hungry wolves.

In the picture on the right there are twelve insects that look like parts of plants. Can you find them all?

A sea anemone hitches a lift with a hermit crab.

A Favour for a Friend

Animals of the same kind often live together and help each other. But it is unusual for two different kinds of animals to do so. Most animals keep well away from crocodiles, but the Egyptian plover knows that it can safely walk all over the dangerous beasts. This is because it feeds on parasites that live on the crocodile's skin. Glad to be rid of the pests, the crocodile even lets the birds peck about inside its great gaping jaws.

The hermit crab has no shell of its own so it lives inside the shell of a dead sea snail. Any sea anemone lucky enough to be attached to the shell is carried around by the crab, and can find more food. The crab's enemies see only the sea anemone and keep clear of the stinging tentacles.

Egyptian plovers 'clean' the teeth of a Nile crocodile.

Animal Homes

Some animals make their homes where they find them, resting briefly under a pile of stones or a heap of leaves. But others work with care and skill to construct more lasting homes.

Nest Builders

Most animals only build a home when it is time to bring up their young. Many birds weave twigs, grass and feathers together to make cup-shaped nests. Others are even cleverer. The tailor bird sews two leaves together and fills them with fluffy plant material to make a warm, soft cradle for its eggs.

The great crested grebe builds a floating nest of reeds.

Living Together

Honeybees live and work together. They build their nest with wax. The nest is a honeycomb of cells. In some cells eggs are laid and grubs reared. In others nectar and pollen are stored so there is always a good supply of food.

The Master Builders

Beavers are always busy building. First they cut down trees with their strong front teeth. They eat the bark and use the wood to make a dam across a stream. A pond of calm water collects behind the dam. In the middle of the pond the beavers build their 'lodge'. The lodge is a platform of twigs and mud that rises out of the water and is covered with a roof of branches. The entrances to the lodge are underwater. Once inside, the beavers are warm and dry and their enemies cannot cross the water to reach them.

Towns Beneath the Prairies

Prairie dogs are small mammals that live on the plains of North America. They build their homes in burrows under the ground.

The 'rooms' of the burrow are lined with straw and connected by tunnels. Each new family adds new burrows to the old ones so that often great underground towns grow up, stretching over many hectares.

The house martin makes a mud nest.

The tailor bird sews its nest with plant fibres.

A weaver bird with its nest of woven grasses.

A song thrush on its basket-shaped nest.

A tiny humming bird with a nest the size of a walnut.

The ringed plover scrapes a hole in the ground to lay its eggs in.

The oven bird's nest is like an old-fashioned oven.

The woodpecker makes its nest by drilling into the trunk of a tree with its beak. The hole may be 30 centimetres deep.

Squirrels nest in dreys high in the trees. The drey is an untidy collection of twigs and moss. The squirrel pushes its way inside and then covers up the entrance hole.

When they are outside feeding, the prairie dogs have to post guards by the entrances to the tunnels to stop snakes getting in. When their enemy the prairie falcon flies over, they all rush underground to escape.

Prairie falcon

Badgers dig deep burrows called sets under the ground. There are several entrances and many tunnels. The 'rooms' are lined with straw. Each spring the tidy badgers throw out the old straw and replace it with new.

A Diving Bell for Baby Spiders

Land animals cannot breathe under water. But even so the water spider builds its home in a pond. First it jumps on the water and catches a bubble of air. Then it dives down and makes a silk web among the waterweeds. It fills the web with bubbles of air until it looks like a dome. Then the female spider lays her eggs in it. The young spiders have plenty of air to breathe when they hatch.

Your Body

Your body is made of millions of tiny cells. It has a covering of skin, and a framework of bones. Inside there are different parts which allow us to move, breathe, speak, eat, and sleep. Our ears, eyes and other senses tell the brain what is going on outside our bodies. The brain controls everything that we do. In fact all the parts of our bodies work together to make the most perfect machine in the world.

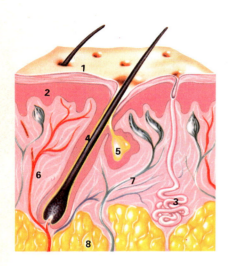

Above is a cut-away view of the skin, showing: 1. Surface 2. Epidermis 3. Sweat gland 4. Hair 5. Sebaceous gland 6. Blood 7. Nerve 8. Fat. The nerve endings in the skin help us to feel cold, hot and pain.

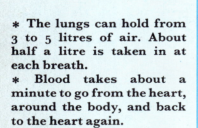

* The lungs can hold from 3 to 5 litres of air. About half a litre is taken in at each breath.
* Blood takes about a minute to go from the heart, around the body, and back to the heart again.
* The skin covering the body measures almost 2 sq. metres.
* We have between 90,000 and 140,000 hairs on our heads.
* An average adult, in one day, drinks about 1.5 litres of liquid and eats about 1.5 kg of food. He breathes about 23,000 times.
* An adult's brain weighs about 1.5 kg.
* If all the blood vessels in a human body were laid end to end they would stretch for nearly 160,000 kilometres.

The Skin
The skin is a waterproof covering that protects the body. It keeps us warm when it is cold and cool when it is hot. It helps us to get rid of waste water by sweating. And it acts as a strong barrier against germs.

The skin is only about a millimetre thick. The part you can see is made of dead cells that flake off all the time. They are too small for us to see. Underneath there are two layers and some fat.

The layer of skin under the surface, has a pattern or ridges and dents. You can see the pattern on your finger tips. The pattern you are born with never changes. And no one else in the world has finger-prints exactly like yours.

Muscles
The joints can only move because they have muscles attached to them, which pull them into the right position. Muscles work in pairs. To raise the lower part of your arm, one muscle contracts (gets smaller) and pulls the bone up. The other muscle is relaxed. To lower your arm the first muscle relaxes and the other one contracts (above).

The Skeleton
If you did not have a skeleton you would be just a flabby blob, unable to stand up. The skeleton is a framework of more than 200 bones, linked by joints. The joints allow us to move. Some work like hinges. The bones at a joint are held together by stretchy ligaments.

Breathing
When you run fast, you sometimes get out of breath. This is because your muscles have used up their oxygen. Oxygen is a gas and is part of the air we breathe in. Without it our bodies cannot work.

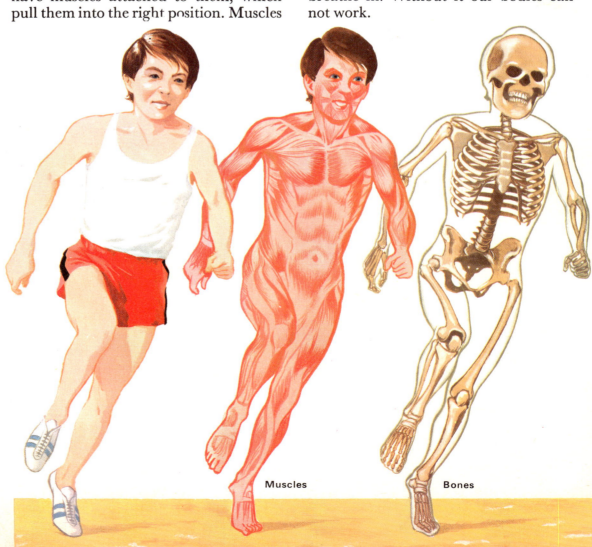

Muscles

Bones

Oxygen is taken into our lungs when we breathe and is carried to all parts of the body by the blood. We would die very quickly without it.

The lungs suck air into the body and blow it out like a pair of bellows. The blood absorbs the oxygen from the lungs and takes it to other parts of the body.

When we breathe out, air passes through a part of the windpipe called the the voice box. Cords in the voice box are pulled taut by muscles. As the air passes by them, the cords vibrate and make sounds. We make the sounds into words by moving our lips and tongues. See what different shapes you make to say your name.

Food and Digestion

We get our energy from the food we eat. The body uses food as fuel. Like petrol in a motor car it has to be 'burned', combined with oxygen, before it can make energy. First it is digested. This means that it is broken down into smaller and smaller bits as it goes from our mouths, through our stomachs to our intestines. The blood collects the food from the intestines and carries it around the body.

Blood

The blood is the body's transport system. It carries oxygen and digested food to all the hungry cells of the body. It carries waste from the cells back to the

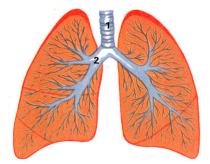

Air passes into the lungs through the trachea (1) and the branching bronchi (2).

lungs and to the kidneys. The blood is pumped round the body by the heart. Nearly 5 litres of blood are pumped by the heart every minute. You can feel the blood moving when you feel the pulse in your wrist.

Brain and Nerves

The brain is the body's control centre. It is connected to every part of the body by nerves. Messages are carried to and from the brain by the nerves. If it gets too dark for you to read this page, nerves from your eyes will inform your brain and the brain will instruct other nerves to tell your muscles to move so that you can put the light on.

Different parts of the brain control different things such as speaking, hearing and seeing. We use our brains to think, and also to 'store' everything that we know.

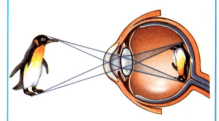

In the centre of your eyes there is a black circle – the pupil. This is in fact a hole, although it has a transparent covering. This allows light into your eye so that you can see. The eye works rather like a camera. Light from the object goes through the lens behind the pupil and throws a picture or image on to the back of the eye. A large nerve carries the information about the image to the brain and the brain tells us what we are seeing. The image on the back of the eye is always upside down but the brain makes us see it the right way up.

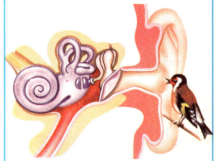

Sounds are vibrations in the air and we hear them with our ears. The part of the ear you can see picks up the vibrations and these make the ear drum inside vibrate, just like the skin of an ordinary drum when it is hit by a stick. The vibrations are passed on to three tiny bones that bang on each other, and pass the vibrations deep inside the ear. There, the vibrations travel around a coiled tube. Tiny nerve cells in the tube pick up the vibrations and send signals to the brain. The brain makes sense of the signals and tells us what the sound is. The ear also helps us to balance.

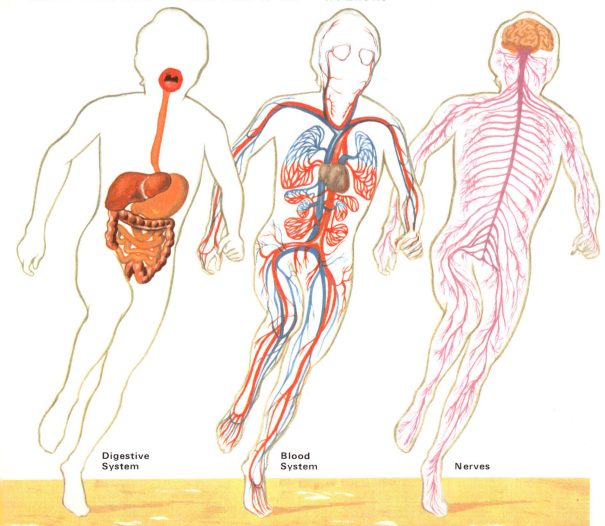

Digestive System

Blood System

Nerves

The polar bear and the walrus live in the far north. The great white bear can creep unseen across the ice, searching for seals to eat. But it will not attack the walrus. It knows to keep clear of those long tusks.

The ptarmigan is an Arctic bird. In winter its feathers are white, so that it can hardly be seen against the snow. As summer comes, the ptarmigan's feathers turn reddish brown.

Eskimos live round the Arctic circle. They kill animals and fish for food, and use animal hides to make warm clothes and tents. The men go fishing in 'kayaks'.

The Lapps also live in the Arctic. Many of them herd reindeer. The reindeer provides the Lapps with meat, milk, cheese and skins for tents, shoes and blankets.

Cold Lands

The coldest places in the world are at the top and bottom of the globe. They are called the polar regions because they lie around the North and South Poles. Very few people live in these vast frozen places.

The Arctic

The northern polar region is the Arctic. It stretches from the North Pole to the Arctic circle – an imaginary line drawn around the globe. At the very North Pole there is no land, only a huge area of frozen sea. When you fly over the North Pole, all you can see is snow and ice. In the summer the edges of this great frozen sea break up; huge icebergs drift south into the Atlantic Ocean and sailors have to keep a close look out for them.

The land in the Arctic region is frozen solid for most of the year. In the short summer the surface soil thaws and some plants can grow, even brightly coloured flowers.

There are now many more people within the Arctic circle than there used to be. This is because valuable minerals have been found there –

minerals such as uranium and iron. Oil has been found in the far north of Canada and the American state of Alaska.

The Antarctic

The continent of Antarctica is a vast cold island at the bottom of the world. It is twice the size of Australia and is always covered by a thick layer of ice which can be as much as 3 kilometres thick. Scientists have found that there are great mountain ranges buried beneath this ice. The Antarctic is much colder than the Arctic. Bitter winds of 160 kph or more are quite common. There are only a very few simple plants.

The seas around Antarctica, however, teem with life. There are whales, seals, penguins, and all kinds of sea birds.

Around the North Pole is a great frozen sea.

The South Pole lies in the middle of Antarctica.

Penguins are birds that cannot fly, but they swim well. They live in the Antarctic. Here are two Emperor penguins with their chick.

The Explorers

The first man to reach the North Pole was an American called Robert Peary. With five companions and sledges pulled by dogs he reached his goal in September 1909. They had to battle for 53 days across piled-up polar ice to reach the top of the world.

The first party to reach the South Pole was led by Roald Amundsen. With 52 dogs to pull their sledges they reached the pole in December 1911.

Captain Robert Scott started for the South Pole only four days after Amundsen. He used man-hauled sledges. When Scott reached the pole after a terrible journey he found a tent set up by Amundsen. The Norwegian had beaten Scott to the pole by a month. Scott and all his men died on the way back.

Today's Polar Explorers

Brave explorers like Captain Scott died because they had very little protection against the freezing Antarctic blizzards. Today's explorers travel across the ice in huge snow-tractors. The tractors pull sledges loaded with food and scientific equipment. Some of these tractors are so big that men can eat and sleep in them.

But even with tractors, travelling in the Antarctic is dangerous. Sometimes great cracks open up in the ice. Tractor drivers must be careful.

The Midnight Sun

It is cold near the North and South Poles because the sun never rises high in the sky. In winter there are days when it does not rise at all. In summer there are days when it can be seen all day and night.

In the polar regions special ships called icebreakers are used to smash a channel of clear water through the pack ice.

There are still many dangers in Antarctic travel. This tractor is trapped in a deep crevasse which has opened up in the ice.

When Captain Scott reached the South Pole he found that the Norwegian Amundsen had got there first. Scott and his men were all frozen to death on their return journey.

Deserts

Deserts are parts of the world that have very little rain. Sometimes years pass without any rain falling. During the day it is usually very hot. At night it can become very cold. Deserts are not easy places for animals and plants to live in.

The Painted Desert
The picture below shows part of a desert in Arizona, USA. It is called the Painted Desert because of the beautiful colours of the rock. The colours change during the day from brilliant blue to yellow and red.

Large areas of the United States are desert lands.

All Kinds of Deserts

When we think of a desert we usually think of sand, miles and miles of sand. But this is only one kind of desert. Even the great Sahara Desert in North Africa is only one-tenth sandy waste. Deserts usually have rocks and pebbles, mountains and valleys. Any large area of dry soil and rocks is a desert.

Why are deserts so dry? Usually they are dry because the winds that blow over them have lost all their moisture. Often a mountain range pushes the wind up high before it reaches the desert. As the wind rises it gets colder and forms rain. This rain falls before the wind gets to the desert. So deserts have dry winds.

By day, a desert is a boiling hot place. There are few clouds to keep out the fierce rays of the sun. At night the desert becomes cold quite suddenly. There is nothing to hold the sun's heat.

Water in the Desert

We call any fertile place in the desert an *oasis*. Some oases are small – just small clumps of palm trees round a pool of water. Others are huge areas like the whole valley of the river Nile. The picture below shows a small oasis in North Africa.

There is always water deep under the earth's surface – even beneath the driest desert. Sometimes the water comes up to the surface and makes an oasis. Caravans with heavily laden camels still travel across the desert, going from oasis to oasis.

Desert Animals

Although the desert is a cruel place to live in, there are many animals that choose to live there. The camel is the biggest of the desert animals. There are two kinds of camel. The one with one hump is called the *dromedary*, and lives in Arabia and Africa. The two-humped camel is the *Bactrian*. It lives in Asia.

The camel can live for months without drinking water. But it needs green vegetation to eat. When a camel is thirsty, it can drink over 100 litres of water in a few minutes. The camel's big padded feet stop it sinking into the sand.

Other desert animals are wild asses, kangaroo rats with long back legs for jumping over the sand, and fennec foxes with their big ears.

There are birds in the desert too. Some fly like the owl. Others like the ostrich and the rhea cannot fly, but they can run very fast.

Animals that crawl along the ground like snakes do not often come into the open during the heat of the day. One snake often found in the American desert is the sidewinder rattlesnake. It can crawl quickly across the loose sand.

The female wolf spider lays her eggs in a silk cocoon shaped like a ball. She carries this cocoon with her wherever she goes.

Can you see all these creatures in the picture on the right?

Desert Plants

Although there is very little water about, plants still manage to live in the desert. Some desert plants have ways of storing water in their stems. Others have very long roots that go deep into the ground to catch every drop of water. Many desert plants have sharp prickles all over them. This is to stop animals from eating them to get at the water inside.

Desert People

People have learned to live in desert areas. Most desert people have dark skins. A dark skin is good protection from the sun's rays. People like the Bedouins, whom you can see in the picture on the left, wear long loose fitting robes. These help to keep them cool. The Bedouins wander from place to place looking for feeding places for their goats and sheep. Their tents are made of skin.

Very old cave paintings have been found in the Sahara. These show that the dry waterless desert was once a green and fertile land. Perhaps some day we will find ways of growing useful crops in the world's deserts.

The World's Deserts
About a fifth of all the world's land is desert. The biggest desert is the Sahara Desert in Africa. There are also big deserts in the Americas and in Asia. Most of the centre of Australia is desert. You can see the world's deserts in the map above. In some deserts it rains only once in ten years.

Jungles and Forests

Forests are large areas of land which are thickly covered in trees. They form one-third of the earth's surface. There are three main kinds of forest, and trees grow everywhere except high on the tops of mountains, in the frozen lands of the Arctic and the Antarctic, and in hot, dry deserts.

Making Sure of the Future

At one time more of the earth was covered by forests than it is now. But over the ages many of them have been cleared away by man to make room for farming land. Today, forests are deliberately planted in certain places so that wood does not become too scarce. These places are called 'forestries' and they are very carefully protected. The trees are sprayed with special chemicals to kill off any harmful insects. Great care must also be taken to see that no fires start.

The wood we get from these forestries has many uses. It not only provides us with fuel and building material, but also with many other things. Some chemicals, paper, rayon and even plastics are made from wood.

Deciduous Forests

Trees which shed their leaves in winter are known as 'deciduous'. The beech, birch, oak, maple and gum are all deciduous trees. Forests of them can be found in most parts of the world where the summers are warm and the winters cool. The hard wood of deciduous trees is used for making furniture, and sports equipment such as bats and oars.

Deciduous forests provide shelter for a great many birds and animals – deer, raccoons, squirrels, badgers, wild cats, grouse and many others. Unfortunately, the deer do a lot of damage to the trees by eating the bark and trampling on young seedlings.

Coniferous Forests

Trees which do not shed their leaves in winter are called 'evergreens'. They have long, thin, needle-like leaves. These trees form their seeds in cones, so they are known as conifers. Coniferous forests are found in parts of the world where the winters are cold, such as North America and parts of Europe and Asia.

On the right you can see some of the creatures which live in coniferous forests. At the bottom of the picture there is a mink which is often hunted for its valuable fur. There are bears, elk, pumas and packs of fierce wolves. The little spiny animal on the branch above is a tree porcupine.

Jungles

The third kind of forest is called a rain-forest or jungle. Rain-forests are found in South America, Africa and parts of the east where it is very hot and there is a lot of rain. Many different kinds of trees grow in rain-forests – teak, banyan, balsa, cypress and mahogany are the most common.

Huge vines tie the trees together and brightly coloured orchids and ferns grow on the branches. Where there is a clearing, perhaps beside a river, the sunlight can filter through the trees. Here the ground is covered in a dense matted undergrowth of ferns, shrubs, palms and brush.

Life in the Jungle

Most jungle animals live up among the trees. The picture on the right shows two long-limbed spider monkeys and some brightly coloured macaws. They hardly ever come down on to the ground. The spotted jaguar takes to the trees when the undergrowth below is too thick for hunting. The giant anaconda snake lives near rivers. It can grow to a length of more than eight metres.

The alligator also lives near rivers. It feeds on other animals like the little opossum which has come down from the trees for a drink.

Jungles are crawling with insects. The ants in the foreground are army ants; they travel in swarms, eating almost anything in their path.

Jungle People

Because so many of the animals live up in the trees, the jungle is not a good hunting ground for the people who live there. Many of the tribes clear small areas and grow crops such as corn, tobacco and pineapples. They trade these crops with produce from other tribes.

The people you see below are called pygmies. They live in the jungles of Africa. They only grow to about 1½ metres tall. While the men hunt for food with their poisonous darts and bows and arrows, the women gather nuts, berries and honey. When the food supply runs low, pygmies move camp to another part of the jungle. But today, they are gradually losing their territory as more and more jungle is being cleared away to make room for roads and cities.

Plantations

Over the centuries, parts of the jungle have been cleared away by settlers. In these clearings, crops such as rubber, tobacco, rice, cocoa and sugar are grown. These places are called 'plantations'.

The picture above is of a rubber plantation. The rubber, in a liquid form called 'latex', is being collected from the rubber trees. The latex is taken to a collecting station where it will be turned into rubber.

Mountains

Almost a fifth of all the world's land is covered by mountains. And most of the high mountains are in groups such as the Himalayas in Asia. Other important mountain ranges are the Rockies and Andes in the Americas and the Alps in Europe.

Mountain Making

Mountains are made by the very slow movements of the earth's crusty surface. These movements can form different types of mountains. There are 'folded' mountains, like the Alps in Europe (picture right). They look like great waves of rock.

'Block' mountains occur where the earth has moved and broken up into huge blocks of rock. The Sierra Nevada in the United States are block mountains.

The famous Black Hills of Dakota are called 'dome' mountains. The look like enormous 'blisters'.

When a mountain is first formed, and at its highest, it is called a 'young' mountain. Mount Everest is a young mountain. It is 8,848 metres high and is the tallest in the world. As the years go by, mountains become worn down by the wind and rain to a medium height of around 2,000 metres. They are then called 'mature' mountains. After millions of years mountains become so worn down that they are little more than rolling hills.

Underwater Mountains

Mountains are not only found on the land, but also under the sea. The ocean bed is covered with mountains, plains and deep valleys. Many islands in the Pacific are really the tips of underwater volcanoes which stick out above the surface of the sea. Huge upheavals have raised them from the sea bed millions of years ago. The highest mountain on earth from its bottom to its top is not really Everest. It is Mauna Kea, on the island of Hawaii in the Pacific. But only about 4,205 metres is above sea-level.

Volcanoes

Some mountains have a hole in their centre. This hole goes deep down into the earth. At the bottom of the hole is red hot liquid rock called *lava*. These mountains are called volcanoes.

When the lava shoots out of the hole at the top of the volcano we say it is *erupting*. With the lava come pieces of rock and ash. As the lava flows down the side of the mountain in a red hot stream it cools and hardens. This is how the mountain is built up over millions of years.

Some volcanoes erupt often, some very seldom and some never erupt at all. These last ones are extinct.

Getting About a Mountain

In the past, mountain ranges have acted as barriers between countries because they were difficult to cross. Modern building methods and inventions have solved this problem. The longest rail tunnel in the world is over 19 kilometres long. It is called the Simplon tunnel and it runs through the Alps between Switzerland and Italy.

Also in the Alps there is a vast network of electric railways. The trains sometimes speed along so fast that passengers say they cannot see the beautiful mountain scenery.

Steep mountain slopes make life for the motorist very difficult. Roads zig-zag their way up in a series of steep sided hair-pin bends. For shorter and easier journeys, many people travel in cable cars. These are small carriages which run along strong wires hung between towers.

Avalanches

The first snow fall of winter brings danger to every living thing on a mountain. The snow piles up on the steep slopes and one slight disturbance can cause it to crash down the mountainside at a frightening speed. This great fall of snow is called an *avalanche*. The destruction it causes can be terrible. On some mountains, special fences have been put up to keep the snow in place. You can see an avalanche in the picture.

Skiing and Climbing

The first skis were probably made thousands of years ago from large animal bones. There is a pair of skis on show in a Swedish museum which are thought to be five thousand years old. Skis have often been used by troops in times of war. But it was not until the early 1800s that skiing first became a sport. Today, millions of holiday makers go each year to ski resorts all over the world.

In ancient times mountains were feared by men and few peaks were climbed before the last century. Mountain climbing has now become a very popular sport. Most of the world's great peaks have been explored and climbed.

Food from the Soil

The number of people that can live on the earth depends on the amount of food that can be grown. To provide food, more people work on the land than at anything else. They are able to grow enough to feed over 5,000 million people.

Everywhere in the world, men till the soil and raise animals for food. Our meat comes mainly from cows, pigs, chickens and sheep.

Less than a hundred different plants account for nearly all the food grown on the land. The most important of all crops are the cereals. Wheat, rice, maize, barley, rye and millet give over half of the world's total food supply. Hundreds of millions of tons of these are produced each year.

Carefully bred farm animals give a great deal more food than their wild ancestors. Cows that are grazed on the best pastures and that are protected from diseases may give 4500 litres of milk a year.

Beehives are often placed in an orchard. The bees gather nectar from the blossoms and store it as honey in their hives.

Where water from wells or springs bubbles to the surface, even the parched desert can be made to bloom. Below: greenhouses trap the sun's heat. In them fruits and vegetables can be grown all year round.

Irrigation has made it possible to farm in even the driest areas. Nearly half the world's farmland is irrigated in some way. Here, a web of ditches brings water to thirsty crops. Below: Using tractors, farmers cultivate vast areas of land.

In large farms helicopters are used to spray crops with insecticides. Many different kinds of diseases and pests can attack crops.

Even the steep slopes of a river valley can be cultivated. Grapes are grown in long terraced rows facing the sun. After the grapes are picked, they are pressed and fermented to make wine.

Many tropical fruits and vegetables are grown on plantations. From top to bottom, workers pick coffee, tea and cocoa. Below: Rice, along with wheat, is the world's most important crop. It is grown in specially flooded fields, called paddies.

Left, top to bottom: Some simple farming tools – flail, pitchfork, hoe, rake, scythe and sickle.
A simple plough.
A wind-driven water pump.
A water-wheel used to work a mill.

Better Plants

Through careful breeding, farmers today can raise more food than ever before. Food scientists have found special kinds of plants that grow faster and are more hardy. Some kinds of wheat give five times as much grain as their wild ancestors. There are kinds of rice that grow so quickly that several crops can be raised where only one grew in the past.

More Meat, Milk and Eggs

Men have bred domestic animals in the same way they have plants. Animals have long been grazed in special pastures or raised in pens where the food was especially rich and plentiful. Here they could also be protected from diseases and harmful insects.

Over the years, those animals that gave the highest quality meat, milk and eggs were picked out for breeding. With time, new varieties of animals arose. These were far healthier and gave more food of a better quality.

Farming with Machines

Machines are taking the place of animals as 'beasts of burden' on farms. In fact, there are so many machines on a modern farm that the farmworker has to know quite a lot about machinery. Tractors are used for pulling all sorts of things – ploughs, drills, and harvesters.

The *combine harvester* is a huge machine that cuts the crop and separates the straw and chaff.

Not all the wild creatures that live around farms are a threat to the crops. The millions of tiny creatures that live in the soil are needed to keep it rich and fertile. They help to decompose dead animals and plants into substances the crops use when growing. Some kinds of bacteria live on the roots of plants. Worms help to turn and loosen the soil with their constant tunnelling. Small rodents and many kinds of birds feed on insects that attack the crops.

Living in a City

The first cities grew up more than 5000 years ago in the East. They were jumbled clusters of flat-roofed houses made of mud. There were stalls and shops. And cities were often ringed by walls. They were places where markets and fairs were held. Merchants and farmers met there and exchanged goods.

Cities have often grown up around good harbours or at river crossings – places where people found it easy to meet and gather. Townspeople lived within the shelter of the city walls. The walls protected them from bandits and wandering armies.

Round the city were fields owned by small farmers and great landowners. Crops and animals were brought into market and exchanged for goods made in the city or brought from far away.

The Cities Grew

As modern industry grew, so did the size of the cities. People crowded into them to work in the new factories. But the cities grew too quickly. People lived

The modern city is a cluster of homes, offices, shops, factories, railways and roads. The picture below shows part of such a city. In the bottom left there is an office block. Part of it is cut away to show the offices and lifts inside. On top is a landing place for helicopters. In the ground under it you can see the building's foundations. Behind this block is the main railway station. Opposite the station are shops, theatres, cinemas, museums and restaurants. Beyond the station you can see a big motorway junction. And to the right of it there are houses, with a sports stadium beyond. Also in the picture you will find a bus station, hotels and factories. Under the ground there are trains and a network of pipes, sewage channels, electric, gas and telephone cables. There is also a road tunnel under the river. Across the river are the docks, with sheds, other factories, and an oil refinery in the distance.

in small, unhealthy houses, often with earth floors. Whole families crowded into a single room. There was no running water and no proper drains. No one collected the rubbish. The streets were unpaved and unlit at night. Diseases were common and they swept through the overcrowded cities. It must have been most unpleasant living in a city two or three hundred years ago.

The Rise of the Modern City

It was not until the 19th century that life in cities began to get better for all the people. Water pipes were laid under the streets, and the streets themselves were paved.

As the cities grew bigger and bigger, people began to travel in trams drawn by horses. Before this the ordinary people had to walk everywhere.

Then came the first underground railways and finally cars and buses. As transport improved, it became easier to move in and out of town. This caused cities to grow even bigger. People began to live in suburbs which ringed the city. They travelled many miles to the city centre to work. With the building of tall office blocks and motorways, cities at last began to look as they do today.

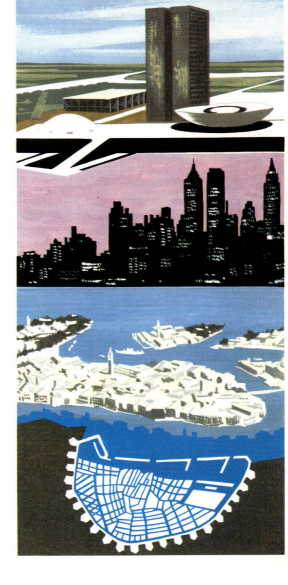

There are all kinds of cities – some old, some new, some rich, some poor. In the East there are cities where many people live on boats in the rivers. There are towns in the Sahara desert where people live in mud-brick houses. There are cities where poor people live in tumble-down shacks in the shadow of big skyscrapers. In the top right picture you can see the modern capital of Brazil, called Brasilia. Below that is the skyline of the the great city of New York. Under that is the old Italian city of Venice, with its canals. On the left is a picture of old London. Notice the houses on the bridge across the river. London today stretches over 30 kilometres.

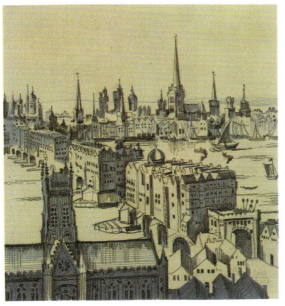

City Planning
The drawing on the right shows how a city is planned. The experts decide where there will be areas of offices, shops, houses and factories. And they work out how they will all be joined up by main roads, smaller roads and railways.

The First Men

The people in this picture look much more like apes than like us. But they are in fact our ancestors. They lived about 2 million years ago.

Scientists have traced our family tree back to ape-like creatures that lived in the forests and moved about on all fours. Very, very slowly our ancestors became more manlike. They started to move on two feet. This meant that their hands were free for making and carrying things. Their brains got bigger and bigger which made them cleverer than other animals. And they learned how to talk.

Man's Ancestors

All that is left of these very early ancestors is some bones. But from them we can build up a picture of them and of how they lived. The people in the picture lived in Africa. They were just over a metre tall. They moved about on two feet, but probably shuffled along rather clumsily.

These early people had no homes. They moved about the country looking for food. They ate seeds, nuts, berries, and roots. Some of them killed and ate animals. But they had to eat them raw since they had no fire. To cut them up they used tools made from pebbles. They chipped away one side of the pebble to make a sharp edge.

Modern Man Appears

The first men who looked really modern had a very hard life. Many places were much colder than now. Some people sheltered in caves. Others made tents of animal skins propped up on branches or huge bones. And some people lived in pits in the ground which they roofed over with branches and earth.

People still had no settled homes. They moved round after the herds of animals – reindeer, bison, and mammoth. Often they would camp in the same place year after year when there was plenty of food there. They hunted animals with flint-tipped spears. They cut up the meat easily with sharp stone cutters. Then they scraped the skins clean. They sewed them together with bone needles to make warm clothes. They probably wore loose tunics and trousers like those of Eskimos. Sometimes they decorated their clothes with rows and rows of little bone beads. They made bone bracelets, and necklaces of bones and teeth.

The man on the right looks much more like us. He lived about a million years ago. He stood really upright and knew how to use fire for scaring away animals, cooking food, and keeping himself warm. This meant that he could live in cool places.

How Early Man Cooked

Meat was roasted over the fire. Men could not make stews because they did not know how to make pots. They heated water by putting it in a skin bag and dropping in hot pebbles. As well as meat, they ate seeds and nuts, berries and roots just like the earlier men in Africa. They fished in the rivers.

These people are men's ancestors. They lived in Africa some two million years ago. Although they look more like apes they are behaving in a man-like way making and using tools, and walking upright.

Some tools fashioned by early men from the stones around them. The earliest ones were crudely chipped, but later ones were shaped by skilfully tapping away thin flakes of the stone. All sorts of shapes were produced from large all-purpose hand-axes to delicate arrowheads.

Early Artists

Men did not know how to make pots of clay. But they used it to make models of animals – bears and lions – and of people. They also carved figures of bone. Sometimes they carved the figures of animals they hunted on rocks near the mouths of caves. Deep inside the caves they painted wonderful pictures of the animals. They drew outlines in black. Then they coloured them in with red, yellow, and brown earths. Sometimes they dipped their hands in the earth and pressed them against the walls to leave handprints. Nobody knows just why they painted these pictures. Perhaps they were a sort of hunting magic.

This way of life came to an end when the weather became warmer. The herds of animals moved away to new cool areas. But men did not follow them. Instead, they learned how to rear animals in fields. They learned how to sow seeds and grow crops just where they wanted them. Now they could settle down and build proper homes. They learned how to make pots by coiling a 'sausage' of clay round and round and then smoothing it over. And they learned how to weave cloth. They had changed from wandering hunters to village farmers.

This painting of a spotted horse comes from deep inside a cave in France. The outline has been drawn in black against a background of pale rock. Above the horse is a hand print. The artist probably put his hand against the wall and then blew powder round it.

People of Long Ago

In prehistoric times people learned about their past through legends. Now we only know about these very early people from the remains of their possessions dug up by archaeologists.

Proper history could not exist until men found out how to write. The Sumerians, people who lived around the great rivers of Mesopotamia, were probably the first to have a written language. But the records of these ancient people tell us very little about how they lived.

The Greeks
It is not until we come to the ancient Greeks that we are able to find out more exactly how ordinary people lived. Greek historians kept careful records of events.

Ancient Science
Ancient peoples first used stone, then copper tools. Then these were replaced by tools of bronze. These simple bronze tools were used to build the great pyramids of Egypt. Iron was not used until later.

The Egyptians had doctors who studied the human body to find out how it works. But the Greeks were the first people to use the science of medicine as we know it.

Ancient Art
But the Greeks were best known as builders, sculptors and poets. They were also good sailors, so they spread their ideas over a wide area.

The Romans followed the Greeks as the rulers of the world around the Mediterranean. They copied much of their art from the Greeks. The Romans are mostly remembered for being great builders and good soldiers and rulers.

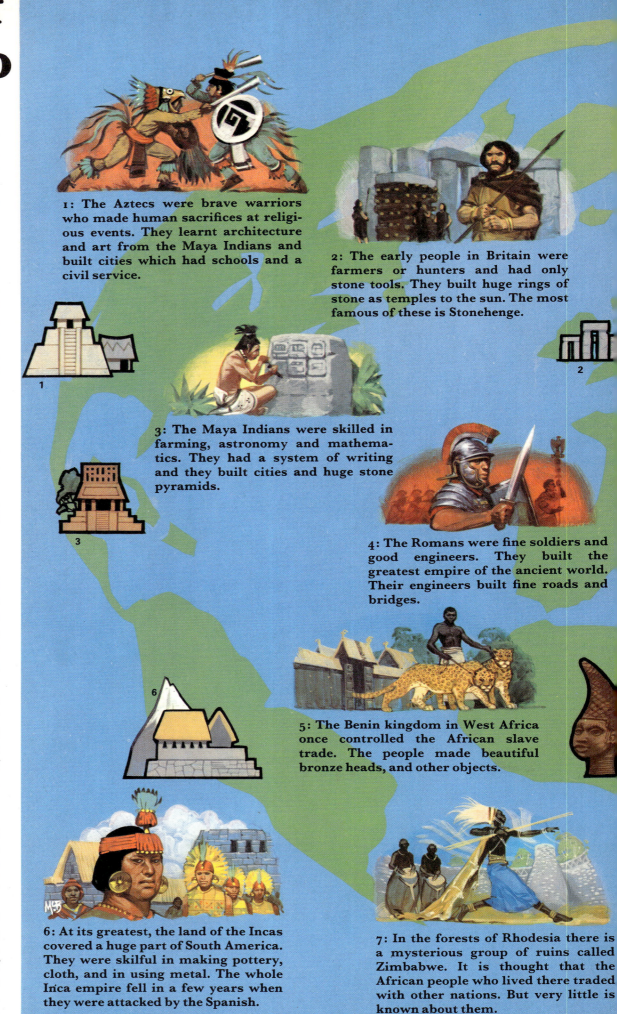

1: The Aztecs were brave warriors who made human sacrifices at religious events. They learnt architecture and art from the Maya Indians and built cities which had schools and a civil service.

2: The early people in Britain were farmers or hunters and had only stone tools. They built huge rings of stone as temples to the sun. The most famous of these is Stonehenge.

3: The Maya Indians were skilled in farming, astronomy and mathematics. They had a system of writing and they built cities and huge stone pyramids.

4: The Romans were fine soldiers and good engineers. They built the greatest empire of the ancient world. Their engineers built fine roads and bridges.

5: The Benin kingdom in West Africa once controlled the African slave trade. The people made beautiful bronze heads, and other objects.

6: At its greatest, the land of the Incas covered a huge part of South America. They were skilful in making pottery, cloth, and in using metal. The whole Inca empire fell in a few years when they were attacked by the Spanish.

7: In the forests of Rhodesia there is a mysterious group of ruins called Zimbabwe. It is thought that the African people who lived there traded with other nations. But very little is known about them.

8: The Phoenicians were known as the Sea People because they traded around the Mediterranean in their ships. They also gave us the alphabet.

9: The great civilization of Ancient China developed from farming communities. They discovered how to print and make silk.

10: Not until the 1940s did modern man first look at a long-forgotten civilization in northern India. It was at Mohenjo-Daro in the valley of the river Indus.

11: The peaceful Minoans grew rich through trading. They built splendid palaces like Knossos where the legendary bull Minotaur lived.

12: The warlike Assyrians had a fine army and horse-driven chariots. Their capital, Nineveh, was a centre of trade and had the first library.

13: The Ancient Greeks are famous as sculptors and writers. They also had the first democracy and started the Olympic Games.

14: The story of the Hebrews is written in the Old Testament. They were farmers who came from Mesopotamia and settled in Palestine. Although they tried to live peacefully, they were constantly invaded by more powerful neighbours.

15: King Hammurabi made Babylon a centre of learning where scholars studied astronomy and mathematics. He wrote the first code of law.

16: The Persians won a huge empire with their strong army and clever generals. When Darius I was king, they built a road 2600 kilometres long from the Mediterranean to the Arabian Gulf.

17: The Egyptians had a civilization that lasted 27 centuries. They used a calender like ours, designed the first clock and made paper. Their engineers built great burial pyramids for the Pharaohs.

18: As long ago as 3000 BC the Sumerians living in the fertile land of Mesopotamia had a written language. They drove in wheeled carriages, used metal and knew how to make pots and weave cloth.

47

Knights and Castles

During the Middle Ages young sons of noblemen trained to be knights. They were taught how to ride, to wear and look after armour, and how to use weapons. They were also taught good manners. When he was old enough, the young man became a squire, the personal servant of a knight. When the squire proved himself in combat, he 'won his spurs'. He knelt before his lord, who dubbed him knight.

Heraldry

In the days when knights wore complete suits of armour it was often difficult to tell friend from foe. So knights took to painting designs on their shields and on the *surcoats* they wore over their armour. These designs came to be called *coats of arms*. They were handed down from father to son.

Some families still have coats of arms which they use as emblems. The study of arms is called *heraldry* and the words used to describe them are in old French. There are words such as *argent* (silver) and *gules* (red).

Knights Jousting

Knights often practised for war at mock combats. These combats were called *tournaments* and they were a most important part of a knight's life.

In the early days of tournaments, many knights were killed. Then strict rules were made. *Jousts* between two opposing knights were often held at the courts of nobles. These jousts were colourful and exciting games staged between famous knights before hundreds of people.

Sometimes riders were knocked off their horses or their lances were shattered – as has happened in the picture below.

Knights wore special armour for these mock combats. It was heavier and less flexible than the armour used in battle. The horses also wore armour.

The picture shows a joust in the early 16th century.

Inside a Castle

In the centre of a castle there was a large courtyard. Round this courtyard were stables for the horses, the shops of the armourer and carpenter. There were barracks for the soldiers and rooms for the castle servants. And there were cookhouses and bakeries.

A castle courtyard was a very busy and noisy place.

The centre of life for the lord of the castle and his family was the great hall. It was a huge room with an enormous roaring fire at one end. At mealtime, servants placed a long trestle table down the middle of the hall. Everyone sat at the table according to their rank, with the lord at the top. They all ate with their fingers from a common dish.

Attacking a Castle

When a castle was under attack, the defenders shot arrows from the battlements and dropped stones and boiling water or oil. The attackers tried to break into the castle in a number of ways. Giant siege towers were wheeled up to the walls and armed men jumped down on to the ramparts.

Powerful catapults hurled great stones or, later, barrels of gunpowder at the walls to try and break them down.

Battering rams were also used to try and smash the walls.

When all these efforts failed, the attackers often found that the only thing they could do was starve the defenders until they were forced out.

Arms and Armour

The first men fought with slings and arrows. Today's weapons include powerful bombs and missiles and huge guns with a range of over 150 kilometres.

Wars in Earliest Times

When the first men disagreed and fought they threw stones at one another. Later they used their hunting weapons for fighting – spears, stone axes, slings and bows and arrows. The first real armies were organized in the Middle East over 5000 years ago. With the invention of the wheel a new weapon – the chariot – was added to battles. Chariots were also used by the Egyptians, as in the picture (right). With them soldiers could plough through the enemy army, letting fly their spears and arrows.

Greek armies used a special tightly-packed formation of men called a *phalanx*. The soldier of the phalanx carried a spear and shield and wore a metal breastplate and helmet.

The great Roman Empire was based on the power of its army. Huge *legions* of about 5000 men marched in long columns across the country. Soldiers mostly fought on foot.

From the Middle Ages to Modern Times

For hundreds of years after the Romans, weapons did not change very much. But armour became heavier and heavier. The fighting man of the Middle Ages was the knight. He was covered from head to foot in a suit of iron and mounted on a strong war horse. But with the invention of gunpowder armour became useless – a ball fired from a musket could pierce even the heaviest suit. Cannons and firearms changed the way wars were fought. Soldiers no longer battled in hand-to-hand combat; they could fire at each other from a distance. Anyone wearing a brightly coloured uniform became an easy target. Soon uniforms were made in dull colours that would not show up easily. These are what soldiers wear today.

Firearms
Today's firearms look very different from their ancestor the cannon. The earliest guns were clumsy to use. If the gunpowder got wet, they could not be fired, so armies only fought in good weather. Today, huge self-propelled guns that look like heavily-armoured tanks can fire shells at targets over 150 kilometres away.

Modern weapons

By the time World War I broke out in 1914, aircraft and motorcars had been invented. We call this war the first truly *mechanized* war, because machines like tanks, planes, and machine guns were used for the first time. Railways carried millions of soldiers to the battlefields, and motor trucks moved supplies quickly overland. The first fighting planes took to the skies, and their pilots became popular heroes.

During World War II even better weapons and machines were produced. Faster, more powerful aircraft carried bombs deep into enemy territory. Submarines fired torpedoes which could sink huge battleships. The biggest land-sea attack took place in June 1944, when hundreds of planes, ships, and tanks were moved across the Channel from Britain to invade France. The first atomic bomb to be used in war was dropped on Hiroshima in Japan.

Since the end of World War II, far more powerful weapons have been built. One of the newest types of atomic weapons needs the older type of atomic bomb just to set it off! Huge missiles can travel thousands of kilometres to bomb a target.

Some famous weapons of World War II:

1. A German 'Stuka' dive bomber, used for blasting tanks.

2. The American Sherman tank

3. Two Browning machine guns

4. An M-40 armoured car

5. A Willys jeep, built to be driven over rough ground.

6. A field gun of the kind used in battles in North Africa.

7. An M1 rifle with bayonet. American bayonets were so long that the soldier could not carry his rifle easily unless he removed the bayonet first.

8. A Thompson sub-machine gun

The Egyptians joined the two ends of their boats with a thick rope. The rope prevented the boat breaking in two when it rode over a wave.

The Greeks and Romans built war galleys with a ram at the front. Two and sometimes three banks of slaves rowed the boats.

In the Middle Ages sailing ships were built with a tall poop at the back to prevent the ship being swamped.

The Story of Ships

The story of ships began in prehistoric times when a caveman first used a floating log to help him cross a river. Today, thousands of years later, sleek ocean liners cross the Atlantic in under four days. Super-tankers three times as long as a football pitch carry millions of gallons of oil in their vast holds. And nuclear-powered submarines can circle the world underwater without coming to the surface.

The oldest pictures of boats are carved in stone on the walls of temples in Egypt. They show that the Ancient Egyptians built boats from bundles of reeds bound together with ropes. Later, wooden planks were used to build bigger and stronger boats called galleys. They were rowed with oars through the water. A large square sail helped to move the galley when the wind was behind it. The Greek and Roman warships were large, fast galleys with an iron ram at the front. They were rowed by two or three banks of oarsmen who were usually slaves.

In the Middle Ages sails replaced oars as a means of propelling a ship. Small, sturdy sailing ships brought goods from distant lands. And sea battles were fought between tall, powerful galleons.

Hydrofoil boats 'fly' through the water at high speeds. As the boat moves forward it is lifted out of the water by underwater 'wings'.

A hovercraft rides over the sea on a 'cushion' of air.

M. TRIM. 76

The clippers were the fastest sailing ships. They carried many sails and had a sharp prow to cut through the waves.

The earliest steamships still carried sails. They were driven by paddlewheels. Today ships are driven by propellers.

When the steam engine was invented, ships no longer had to rely on the wind. And steam engines could move larger, heavier vessels than sails. Huge ships built of iron gradually replaced wooden sailing ships.

The last of the great sailing ships were the graceful clippers which carried tea from China. Designed for speed, the clippers carried three, four and even five tall masts of billowing sails. It was many years before steamships could sail as fast as a clipper in a good wind.

For hundreds of years sea battles were fought between heavily armed galleons. Some carried more than one hundred guns. The gunners aimed at the waterline of an enemy ship so that the sea would rush in through the hole made by the cannonball. They also aimed at the masts to bring the sails down and leave the enemy ship helpless.

At night ships carry white lights on the fore and main masts. On the port (left hand) side they have a red light. On the starboard (right hand) side they carry a green light. By looking at the pattern of lights sailors can tell in which direction a ship is sailing.

Trains and Railways

George Stephenson's Rocket won a competition held in 1877 to choose the best locomotive for a new railway line. Later steam locomotives may have looked very different from the Rocket but they worked in much the same way.

Below, Robert Stephenson's Patentee locomotive which ran on the Liverpool and Manchester Railway in 1834.

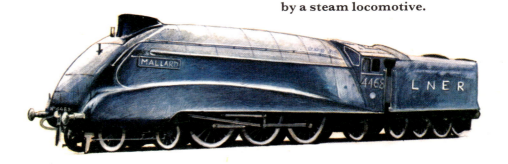

Two hundred years ago travel by road was uncomfortable and very slow. In summer, carriage axles broke on the rutted, dusty road. In winter, the wheels sank in deep pools of mud. And there was always the danger of being held up by highwaymen.

When the steam engine was invented several people tried to build a steam-driven road carriage. But none was successful on the bad roads. Then a British engineer, Richard Trevithick, hit upon the idea of mounting a steam carriage on rails to give a smoother ride.

The idea of making a track for the wheels of vehicles was not new. The Ancient Greeks cut smooth grooves in their roads for the wheels of chariots. Much later, iron tracks were used in coal mines to make the ladened wagons move more easily. But with the invention of the steam engine railways completely changed travel on land.

The first public railway to use steam locomotives was the Stockton and Darlington line in Northern England. It was opened in 1825. George Stephenson, a self-taught engineer, built the ten-mile track and its first engine, called *Locomotion*. A few years later Stephenson built his most famous locomotive, *The Rocket*.

The railway age had begun. Within 25 years there were railways in most European countries, and enough track

In 1936 a streamlined British locomotive, the Mallard, reached a speed of 203 kilometres per hour. This record has never been broken by a steam locomotive.

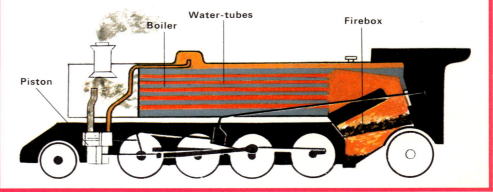

In a steam locomotive coal is burned in the firebox. Water running through tubes in the boiler is heated by the burning fuel and turns to steam. Steam takes up much more space than water and the pressure in the boiler increases. Steam is allowed to escape from the boiler by moving a piston in a cylinder. The piston in turn moves the driving rod, which turns the wheels of the locomotive.

Boiler

Water-tubes

Firebox

Piston

Huge diesel locomotives haul goods wagons on the long journey across America.

those used in large trucks. Electric locomotives are driven by powerful electric motors. They are connected to an electricity supply by overhead wires or by a third 'live' rail.

Until the beginning of this century the railways had no rivals. Then the motor car and the aeroplane were invented. Railways were used less and less and some lines closed. Now, new trains are being built which travel twice as fast as a car. And hover-trains which glide on a cushion of air have been invented. The railways of the future will be faster and more comfortable than ever before.

had been laid to stretch around the world. It was not long before people and goods could travel right across North America, Europe and Asia by rail.

Bigger and more powerful steam locomotives were built over the years. But they all worked in much the same way as the early engines. Coal burning in a firebox heated water and turned it to steam. The pressure of the steam forced large pistons to and fro in cylinders. The pistons were connected to the driving wheels and turned them round.

Steam locomotives belching smoke hauled passenger trains and goods wagons for over one hundred years. But there are few left today. They have been replaced by diesel and electric locomotives which are cleaner, quieter and cheaper to run.

Diesel locomotives are powered by oil-burning diesel engines similar to

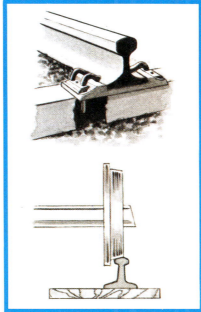

The wheels of locomotives and carriages are specially shaped to run on the curved surface of a rail. A flange on the inside of each wheel makes sure that it does not leave the rail,

Electric locomotives have travelled at 330 kilometres per hour on straight stretches of track. They are clean and quiet.

The French Aerotrain is a hover-train which speeds along a rail on a cushion of air. It is powered by a gas turbine engine similar to the engines used in jet aircraft. The Aerotrain has travelled at 375 kilometres an hour and is the world's fastest train.

The Motor Car

The car is almost as much a part of our lives as the furniture in our house. We take it for granted. It takes us from place to place provided we put petrol into it. Sometimes it goes wrong, but that doesn't happen very often.

We should remember however that it was only about 50 years ago that people began using cars as we do. Then there were few cars on the roads. And cars then were more difficult to drive and less comfortable.

In another 50 years the cars of the 1970s will look very odd to you.

The Right Speed

Cars are pushed along by either their front or back wheels. The engine is usually at the front.

As the engine's pistons go up and down they turn the crankshaft. The crankshaft is joined to the *clutch* and the *gear-box*, as you can see in the picture.

If you have a bicycle with gears you will know what a gear is. In top gear you can go fast while turning the pedals quite slowly. In bottom gear you have to turn the pedals more quickly, but it is easier to go up hill. The same happens in a car. If the driver wants as much power from the engine as he can get, he uses a low gear. He wants plenty of power for starting off or going up a steep hill. If he drives along a clear, straight road he will use top gear.

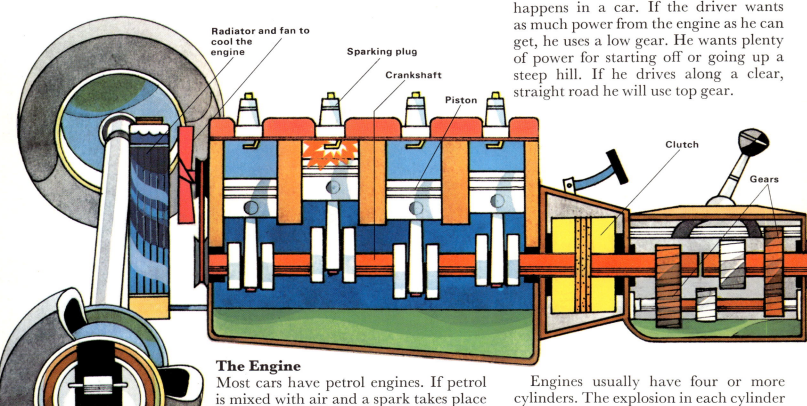

Radiator and fan to cool the engine

Sparking plug

Crankshaft

Piston

Clutch

Gears

Brakes

When a driver wants to slow down or stop the car he presses the brake pedal. The brakes act on all four wheels. The hand brake acts only on the back wheels. It is used to keep the car from rolling when it is stopped.

The Valves

Holes called valves at the top of the cylinders must open and close at just the right moment. These valves let in the petrol and let out the used gas. The spark must also happen at just the right time if the engine is to work properly.

The Engine

Most cars have petrol engines. If petrol is mixed with air and a spark takes place in the mixture, it explodes. This is what happens in a petrol engine. The explosion is made to turn the wheels of the car.

On the right is a picture of part of an engine. You can see a *cylinder*, which is a wide tube. Inside the cylinder is a *piston*, which exactly fits inside the cylinder, and moves up and down in it.

A mixture of petrol and air is drawn into the top of the cylinder. The piston moves down. (Picture 1).

The piston moves up and squeezes the petrol and air mixture. (Picture 2).

A spark is made to take place in the top of the cylinder. This makes the petrol and air explode. The explosion pushes the piston down. (Picture 3).

The piston moves upwards again and the used gas is pushed out of the cylinder. (Picture 4). Then more petrol and air is sucked in and we start again.

The driver can make the car go faster by pressing the *accelerator* pedal. This makes more petrol go into the cylinders.

Engines usually have four or more cylinders. The explosion in each cylinder takes place at a different time. When one piston is going down, another is going up. You can see in the picture above how each piston is joined to the *crankshaft*. As each piston goes up and down it helps to turn the crankshaft, just like a cyclist's legs turning the pedals of a bicycle.

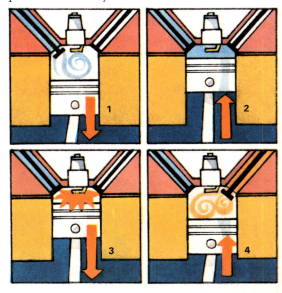

The Story of the Car

The first real motor cars were made in Germany nearly 100 years ago. They looked rather like horse-drawn carriages without the horses.

But it was in the United States that people began making cars in large numbers. Between 1908 and 1927 a man called Henry Ford built factories that made 15 million cars. They were called *Model T* Fords and they looked like the car on the right. Henry Ford was the first man to use what we call an *assembly line*. In an assembly line the cars are put together part by part as they move down a line of workers.

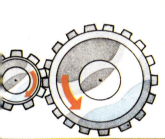

The two wheels with teeth are gear wheels. The small wheel has 9 teeth, the big wheel 18. If the small wheel is driving the big wheel, the big wheel will turn at only half the speed of the small one.

The electric car above can run for a few hours at a slow speed. One of the main troubles with the petrol engine is that it gives out gas that poisons the air we breathe. The electric engine is quiet and it doesn't make poisonous gas. But it has to run on batteries. No one has yet invented a battery that is light enough and will give enough power.

Some people think that the car of the future will look something like the one below.

Turning the Wheels

Some cars have *automatic transmission*. This means that the engine changes gear itself when it reaches certain speeds. The driver does not have to change gear unless he wants to go backwards.

The clutch is only a way of cutting off the engine from the gear-box. When the driver presses the clutch pedal he separates the turning crankshaft from the gears. Then he can safely change into any gear he wants. Most cars have four forward gears, and one to make the car go backwards.

Behind the gear-box is a long rod that runs right to the back of the car. This rod turns at the speed the driver wants. (He uses his gears and the accelerator to do this.) The rod turns other gears on the axle between the back wheels. So the back wheels are made to drive the car at the speed the driver wants.

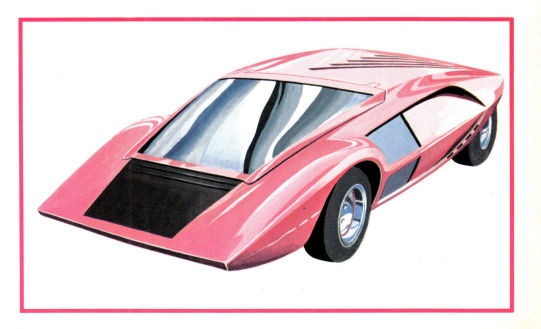

The Story of Aircraft

People have always wanted to fly like the birds. Over the ages many have tried to fit themselves with wings and fly. But people cannot keep themselves in the air by using their own muscles to flap wings.

The Chinese were flying kites before 200 BC. It was by looking at kites and finding out what made them fly that people began to build gliders.

Two young American brothers called Orville and Wilbur Wright were very interested in gliders. In the year 1903 they went to some sand dunes with one

The Wright brothers making the first ever powered flight.

The first powered flight in Europe was made in 1906 by a Brazilian called Alberto Santos-Dumont. His plane was called the 14-bis, and it flew tail first.

In 1909 Louis Bleriot became the first man to fly across the English Channel. He landed at Dover after a flight lasting 37 minutes.

A three-winged Fokker fighter of World War I. The plane was flown by many of the German air aces.

The Short Empire flying-boats took off from and landed on water. Before World War II they flew passengers to Africa and the Far East.

The DC-3, sometimes called the Dakota, was one of the great early airliners. Over 10,000 of them were built, and some of them are still flying.

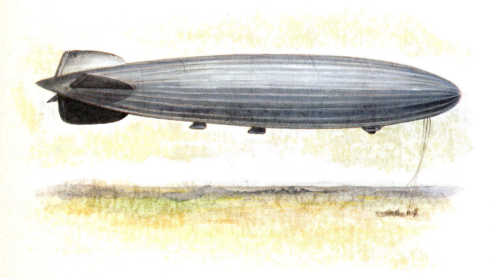

Lighter than Air

The first men to leave the ground were carried up in a balloon made by the Montgolfier brothers in France. The brothers had found out that hot air rises. So they filled a big bag with heated air and let it go. It rose into the air.

Then men found out that bags filled with hydrogen gas would rise, just like hot air balloons. Hydrogen is a gas that is lighter than air.

Balloons had to go where the wind took them. But airships had engines and propellers, so they could be steered. The most famous airship maker was the German Count von Zeppelin. He made many huge airships during World War I, some of which dropped bombs on England. After the war the great 'Zeppelins' carried passengers across the oceans. But the big airships were hard to handle. When the Zeppelin 'Hindenburg' exploded and burst into flames, killing 36 people, that was the end of the monster airships.

of their gliders. But this glider was different. It had a petrol engine which worked a propeller. The brothers had even built the engine themselves. Orville got into this strange machine and the engine was started. With Wilbur running after it, the plane rose a few metres into the air and stayed up for about 12 seconds. This flight by the Wright brothers was the first ever by a powered aircraft.

In 1909, Louis Bleriot became the first man to fly across the English Channel. The Frenchman became world famous after his dangerous 37-minute flight.

When World War I began in 1914 there were no real fighting planes. But soon brave pilots were fighting each other in the skies over France and bombers were dropping bombs.

After the war there were many famous flights. Perhaps the most famous was the first one-man crossing of the Atlantic in 1927. The daring American, Charles Lindbergh, made the flight in a plane with no radio and no parachute. He had thrown everything away to save weight. Lindbergh kept falling asleep during the long flight, but after flying for 33 hours he landed safely in Paris.

World War II saw the first flights of many famous planes. There were the British Spitfires and the German Messerschmitts that fought the Battle of Britain. And later in the war the first jet plane appeared.

Now people fly all over the world in huge jumbo jets, and Concordes that fly faster than the speed of sound. A great deal has happened in the years since the Wright brothers flew that first little hop.

The German Otto Lilienthal learned about flying by making gliders. He hung below his early machines and controlled them by swinging his body. He was almost ready to fit an engine to his strange craft when he crashed and was killed.

The Hawker Hurricane fighter was in service with the RAF when war broke out in 1939. It shared the honours in the Battle of Britain with the Spitfire.

The Boeing 747 'jumbo jet' was the first of the very big airliners. It can carry over 400 passengers in comfort.

The Russian Mil Mi-6 is one of the largest helicopters in the world. It can lift loads of nearly 40 tonnes.

The Lockheed SR-71A is the fastest jet in the world. It can fly at 3540 kilometres per hour and has been up to a height of 30 kilometres.

Concorde takes off, looking like some strange bird. This fast airliner flies at twice the speed of sound. It takes only $3\frac{1}{2}$ hours to cross the Atlantic. The plane was designed and built jointly by the British and the French.

Into the Future

What will life be like in the future? This is a very difficult question.

Some things are certain to change. For instance, the earth's supplies of oil and gas and coal are going to run out before very long. Already people are looking for new sorts of power. They are building huge windmills which will drive machines and make electricity. And they are building special roofs which trap the sunlight to heat water.

More and more people are being born each year. Farmers and scientists are already looking for new ways of producing food to feed them all.

These changes are easy to foretell. But think how quickly things can change. Fifty years ago television and plastics were just being invented. Who can guess what difference today's inventions will bring?

In the future, spacecraft and satellites of all kinds will be launched in space from big orbiter craft. The picture above shows the orbiter launching a satellite. The satellite will stay up in space to relay radio and television signals. The orbiter will return to earth and land, just like an ordinary plane.

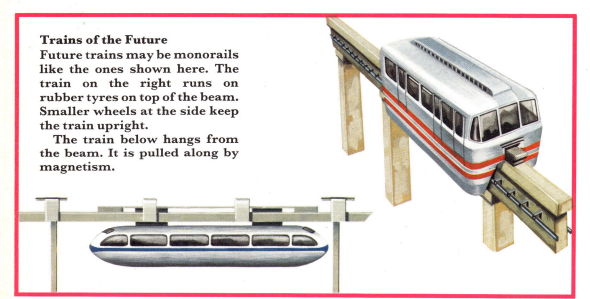

Trains of the Future
Future trains may be monorails like the ones shown here. The train on the right runs on rubber tyres on top of the beam. Smaller wheels at the side keep the train upright.

The train below hangs from the beam. It is pulled along by magnetism.

Cars of the future may look something like the one below. Some people think that cars will have 'electronic brains'. These will allow the car to drive itself down a road in perfect safety. The 'brain' will steer the car as it is directed by magnetic signals sent out from a cable buried under the road.

Index